Relation and Consciousness
A Logical System of Metaphysics

Eric Toms

1984
SCOTTISH ACADEMIC PRESS
EDINBURGH

First published in Great Britain, 1984
by Scottish Academic Press Limited,
33 Montgomery Street, Edinburgh EH7 5JX.

© 1984 Eric Toms

ISBN 0 7073 0435 0

British Library Cataloguing in Publication Data

Printed by Clark Constable, Edinburgh, London, Melbourne

CONTENTS

ACKNOWLEDGMENTS

The short work presented here is the outcome of many earlier versions which proved to be faulty or fallacious in various ways. Those chiefly responsible for aiding me through this tangled skein are Mr Patrick Shaw of the University of Glasgow, Prof. Timothy Sprigge and Dr Noel O'Donoghue of the University of Edinburgh, and my wife Joanne. I thank all these kind helpers for their comments, support and encouragement, especially Pat whose comments were a valuable guide in the final revision, and Joanne for her interest in the subject-matter and her readiness to discuss the texts with me as they developed. I would also like to thank all at the Scottish Academic Press and Clark Constable Printers for their excellent production of the book. No doubt errors remain, but the responsibility for these is solely mine.

PART I

THEORY OF RELATION

1. *The Birth of the System*

The two topics, relation and consciousness, are connected in this essay by a single aim, *viz.* to resolve the issue between idealism and materialism by a study of the relation between consciousness and matter. To this end, I first study relation in general, afterwards applying the result to the special case of the relation between consciousness and matter.

It was not my original intention to work in terms of an axiom system. I was driven to do so on account of accusations of begging the question. The outcome, which I call the 'System', comprises abbreviations, definitions, axioms, and theorems. I avoid symbols, and mete out the System in small doses, interspersing it with elucidation and comment.

In the later stages of work on the System, I found that theorems could be formulated not only about relation in general, but also about relation in application to consciousness. I therefore decided to extend the System and maintain the same method of treatment throughout, *viz.* by the statement and discussion in sequence of suitably small sections of the System. At the same time there is a plain enough distinction between the general treatment and the special application. Part I contains the general treatment, concluding with T9. Part II contains the special application, T10-T19.

In the following formulation of the System (for reference) only sketches of the proofs of theorems are given. Full proofs are given later, in the contexts in which the theorems are discussed. I add two notes on the statement of proofs:

(1) It is a well known truth of elementary logic that from the statement 'If p is the case then q is the case' we can infer 'If q is not the case, then p is not the case'. For this inference, which I frequently refer to in the text, I use the logician's word 'transposition'.

(2) I use the word 'reductio' for 'reductio ad absurdum', which means 'proof by reducing to a contradiction the opposite of the statement to be proved'.

The System

Abbreviations

1. 'A and B are communal' for 'A and B have some content in common' (*i.e.* numerically the same content).
2. 'A and B are simply different' for 'A and B have no content in common'.
3. 'A is discrepant from B' for 'Some content of A is simply different from B'.
4. 'Difference-in-identity' for 'Difference compatible with identity'.

Definitions

D1. A term is whatever is 'continuously' one, *i.e.* whatever has no content(s) unrelated in it to any of the remaining content(s).

D2. A system is a term containing two or more terms.

D3. A relation between two terms is indirect if and only if it contains some term simply different from each of the related terms.

D4. A relation between two terms is direct if and only if it does not contain any term simply different from each of the related terms.

Note on D4. From D4, a direct relation is, by A2 below, contained in its terms:

either (1) wholly in one term,

    or (2) partly in one term and the remaining part in the other,

    or (3) wholly or partly in both terms.

In cases (1) and (2) the terms are not implied to be communal, and the relation is said to be 'semi direct'. In case (3) the terms are implied to be communal, and the relation is said to be 'fully direct'.

Axioms

A1. For any three terms X, Y, and Z, if X contains Y and Y contains Z, then X contains Z.

A2. Any term not contained in a given term is discrepant from it, and conversely any term discrepant from a given term is not contained in it.

A3. A relation between two terms is 'continuous' (or a 'continuity') from one term to the other, *i.e.* no gap of unrelatedness occurs in passing from one term to the other via the relation. Conversely, continuity from one term to another constitutes a relation between them.

A4. If one term contains another without being discrepant from it, the two are identical.

A5. Consciousness exists (not used until Part II, T13).

Theorems with sketches of proofs. Part I.

T1. Any term contains itself.

> *Proof.* By reductio, using A2.

T2. Any two terms of a system are related in the system.

> *Proof.* By reductio, using A3 to separate two groups of terms in the 'system', and then applying D1 and D2 to show that the result is not a system.

> *Corollary.* Any two contents of a term are related in the term.

T3. Two communal terms are directly related.

> *Proof.* By T1 and D2, a term and a content of it form a system, and so by T2 are related (Cor. 1 below). By A3 we then combine two relations of *containing* and obtain Cor. 2. The theorem then follows because the terms alone of a community relation are sufficient to ensure community.

> *Cor. 1.* If one term contains another, the two are related.

> *Cor. 2.* Two communal terms are related.

> *Cor. 3.* Two communal terms are in fully direct relation (see note on D4).

T4. Any relation is a term.

> *Proof.* By comparing A3 with D1.

T5. Two directly related terms are communal.

> *Proof.* In the step from a term to a simply different

term, there has to be a change. This is simply different from each term. Hence the relation is indirect. The theorem follows by transposition of this result. Used in proof: A1, A3, D3, D4.

> *Cor.* Semi direct relations are impossible.

T6. Indirect relations are impossible.

> *Proof.* In an indirect relation, the series of intermediate terms could be infinite only if there were always a gap of unrelatedness in the total relation, which contradicts A3. Hence successive relations in the series have no intermediate terms, and so are direct, and by T5 the successive terms are then communal. But the development of D3 shows that successive terms are simply different.

T7. Two related terms are communal.

> *Proof.* At once from T5 and T6.

T8. Two communal terms are identical.

> *Proof.* The supposition that one of the two terms contains something not contained in the other is reduced to absurdity. Using A2 and A1, T7 transposed shows that this term splits into two unrelated parts, which by T2 is impossible. Identity follows by A4.

T9. Two related terms are identical.

> *Proof.* At once from T7 and T8.
>
> *Cor.* All continuity is identity.

Theorems with sketches of proofs. Part II.

T10. A term at any time of its existence is identical with itself at any other time of its existence.

> *Proof.* By D1 and T9.
>
> *Cor. 1.* No term can gain or lose any content during its existence.
>
> *Cor. 2.* Any two terms must be either always communal or always simply different.

T11. Two terms which can be related must coexist, and be identical throughout their existence.

> *Proof.* By T7 the terms cannot be simply different, and so must be communal, and by T8 identical. Identity at all times, and hence coexistence, are then proved by T10.

Cor. Two terms which can (ever) be related must be related at all times of their existence.

T12. Any one existence is one term.

Proof. By aligning the meaning of 'one' in 'one existence' with the meaning of 'one' given in D1.

T13. Consciousness is one existing term.

Proof. From knowledge of the unity and existence of a state of consciousness (A5), which is then one term by T12. Different states are related, and hence identical by T9.

T14. Every term must coexist with consciousness, and be identical with it throughout their existence.

Proof. By reductio, showing (by T13, T12, T2, T3 Cor. 2, A3) that the unrelatedness of something to consciousness implies its relatedness to consciousness at a certain time (now), and hence by T11 that there is identity and coexistence at all times.

Cor. 1. Any two terms must coexist and be related and identical throughout their existence (by applying A3).

Cor. 2. Any difference between terms must be difference-in-identity.

T15. Whatever exists must be one term, and must always be consciousness.

Proof. By reducing to contradiction the supposition of a gap of unrelatedness, using T2 transposed, T14 Cor. 1, D1, T14.

Cor. So long as anything exists, consciousness exists.

T16. Something must always exist.

Proof. An actual state of nothingness would be a real, distinctive condition of reality, *i.e.* it would be an existence.

T17. Consciousness must always exist.

Proof. At once from T16 and T15 Cor.

T18. No non-conscious thing can exist.

Proof. By reductio, applying T15.

T19. Consciousness is infinite.

Proof. By T18 no absolute limit to consciousness is possible.

Cor. Consciousness can be limited only by itself.

2. *Main Features of the System*

I shall discuss two main features of the System, *viz.* the distinction between direct and indirect relations, and the prominence of community (having something in common).

Traditionally idealism has been supported through a study of relations by first distinguishing between 'internal' and 'external' relations, and by then showing that, despite the common assumption of the reality of external relations, there are strictly no such relations. The same general plan is followed here. So far as the first Part of the System is concerned (up to T9), we do however claim to go beyond the tradition with respect to logical accuracy, and hence with respect to the force of the proof that there are no external relations. We shall see too that the proof goes considerably further than the elimination of external relations.

An internal relation is a relation such that, given the two terms alone, the relation is fixed. For example, given two rods A and B, their relative lengths are fixed. Let us suppose that A is in fact double the length of B. Then the rods themselves are sufficient to determine that A is double the length of B, and nothing apart from the rods is needed to determine this. Naturally, then, a relation of relative length is said to be 'internal' to its terms. An external relation, on the other hand, is a relation such that, given the two terms alone, the relation is not fixed. For example, given two physical things A and B, the distance of A from B is not fixed. It may be five metres, but it could be a hundred metres, with (presumably) just the same two terms. In such a case the relation seems obviously not determined by what the terms themselves are, and so it is naturally said to be 'external' to them.[1]

Now since an external relation is not determined by what the terms are, something other than the terms is needed in order to determine what the relation is. The point is a simple one, but tends to be overlooked in discussions about external relations. The consequence of it is that an external relation between two terms requires something other than the terms

[1] This classification follows David Hume, *A Treatise of Human Nature*, London 1911, Bk. I, Pt. III, section 1.

themselves in order to relate them in this way. This means that an *intermediate term* is required, and that the relation is accordingly *indirect*. An external relation is an indirect relation, and an indirect relation can be precisely defined by interpreting this requirement of an intermediate term in terms of the clarified vocabulary of the System (see D3).

Correspondingly, an internal relation does not need any intermediate term, and so is direct. What is needed to relate the terms of a direct relation must be wholly within the terms themselves. But since there are *two* terms, what does this mean? Does it mean that what is needed for the relation is wholly (or partly) in both terms? Or does it mean that it is wholly in one term? Or does it mean that it is partly in one term and partly in the other? On the first alternative I say that the relation is 'fully direct' (see D4, case 3). On the other two alternatives I say that the relation is 'semi direct' (see D4, cases 1 and 2), since although what is needed to relate the terms is indeed within the terms, it is nevertheless other than one of them, or in part other than one and in part other than the other. A semi direct relation thus retains something of the character of an indirect relation, although it is direct.

By interpreting the distinction between internal and external relations in terms of the distinction between direct and indirect relations, we thus come upon the further distinction between semi direct and fully direct relations. This is important because, as we shall see later, the validity of the System depends crucially upon whether we can prove the impossibility of semi direct relations.

The second main feature of the System is the stress laid upon community (having something in common). The main theorem T7 (the 'Relation Theorem') is that two related terms are communal. It follows at once from T5 and T6. Of these two, T6 has a proof which is mathematical in character, and not, I think, likely to be disputed. It formalises (with additions) Bradley's famous argument about external relations.[1] But the proof of T5 is philosophical in character. I do not see how T5 could be false, but I have found it very difficult to prove. The Relation Theorem has its historical counterpart in one of

[1] F. H. Bradley, *Appearance and Reality*, 2nd ed., London, 1920, p. 21.

Spinoza's Propositions, which (transposed) claims that two *causally* related terms are communal.[1]

The 'Identity Theorem' (T9) is that two related terms are *identical*. Community, of course, already involves identity in qualified form, and because of this it serves in the System as a stepping stone to identity. From the implication of community (by any relation) in T7, we go on in T9 to the implication of unqualified identity. Though very difficult to believe, T9 thus follows at once from T7 and T8. Moreover, the proof of T8 is formally straightforward, so the burden of proof for T9 is bound to fall on T7; and finally on T5 since, as I indicated above, the proof of T6 is also formally straightforward.

But critics of T5 are still in a difficulty, for how are they to make sense of semi direct relations, which must be admitted if T5 is rejected? Although T5 may be hard to prove, it does seem obviously true; and yet it leads on by simple logical steps to T9, which is very difficult indeed to believe. In view of this peculiar situation, a persistent critic would probably still question T5, in spite of its near certain truth. For this reason, adequate proof of it is essential.

Of Part II, I shall say very little at this stage, except to draw attention to two proofs of a philosophical character, *viz.* the proofs of T14 and T16. The second depends upon a profound logical principle, which I call the 'affirmativeness of negation'. The proof of the other, T14, is a general proof of monistic idealism, which in one form or another has occurred repeatedly in the history of philosophy. What distinguishes the proof as given in the text is its clear reductio ad absurdum form, made possible by its context in the System and by formulating the precise proposition for rejection.

3. *Content.* A1, A2, A4

The importance of the notion of community presupposes the importance of the notion of containing (or content). For to say that two terms are communal is to say that they have at least one common content.

The definition of a term (D1) already refers to the content of

[1] B. Spinoza, *Ethics*, New York, 1949, Pt. I, Prop. 3.

a term. But it is the axioms A1 and A2 which give us the working properties of the notion of content.

For the purposes of illustration, we can treat the following as terms: things, persons, events, actions, thoughts. All these have parts. They also have qualities and structure. Typical contents of a term can be taken, again for illustrative purposes, to be its parts, qualities and internal structure.

I stress that such assumptions are only for illustrative purposes (in case the reader finds a notion like *containing* somewhat abstract). For nothing of this can be assumed, without further justification, in proofs. Least of all can we assume that a certain quality *as universal* is a content, since this might result in begging the issue of realism versus nominalism. Nor, obviously, can we assume in proofs, that any particular relational property is a content of a term, since this might beg the main theorem, *viz.* T7, the Relation Theorem.

However, as the illustrations suggest, there are probably very different sorts of contents. At the same time there is a general sense of 'in' which alone justifies the inclusion of any special sort. It is this general sense which enables us to see the truth of the relevant axioms.

A1 is surely self-evident as it stands, and is surely a logical consequence of the general sense of 'in'. To make its self-evident character still clearer, we might express it in the form 'If X contains Y, then it contains every content of Y'. That is, to contain something is, strictly, to contain everything that there is in it.

The converse of A1 is equally self-evident. It can be expressed by negating both antecedent and consequent of the form of A1 just stated. We then have: 'If Y is not contained in X, then some content of Y is not contained in X'. A2 resembles this, but goes further. Bearing in mind the meaning of 'discrepant' given in Abbreviation 3, what A2 says is: 'If Y is not contained in X, then some content of Y is *simply different* from X' (*i.e.* has nothing in common with X). Of course, the content of Y which is simply different from X would not, in general, be the same content of Y as the content of Y which is not contained in X.

In any case, why introduce simple difference at all? The answer is that the statement 'A is not contained in B' does not, by itself, tell us the kind of factual condition that would make the statement true. We know theoretically that it is supposed to contradict 'A is contained in B', but we are not given a respect, or means, by which the contradiction of it is effected. But if we replace it by the equivalent statement 'A has some content simply different from B', we know at once what to look for in A, to ensure that the statement 'A is contained in B' is contradicted.

For this reason it turns out that the notion of simple difference has an indispensable role to play in the System, in spite of the fact that it is eventually proved incapable of objective existence (T14). It gives a precision and effectiveness not attainable by the notion of *not containing*. This is why, for example, the word 'discrepant' is defined in terms of simple difference rather than in terms of *not containing*, and why indirect relations (D3) and direct relations (D4) are similarly defined in terms of simple difference. A2 thus has the important function of transforming propositions involving the unfruitful notion of *not containing* into propositions involving the fruitful notion of simple difference.

A glance at Abbreviations 1-3 shows that community, simple difference and discrepancy are all defined in terms of *containing*. If we now place *containing* along with these three defined notions, we have four notions, which very plainly correspond with the four relations between classes, in terms of which the Aristotelian categorical syllogism is commonly interpreted. This suggests that there is a thorough-going analogy between the notion of a

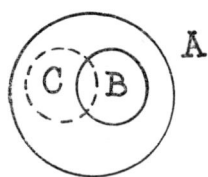

term (in the System) and the notion of a class. We can, indeed, represent relations between terms by diagrams, as we can relations between classes. But we must be careful not to read too much into such diagrams. For example if A has content B, we might think that B divides A neatly into the contents belonging to B, and all other contents of A, just as a class can be divided into the members of an included class and all the other members of the class. But if we consider any other content C of A, it might be communal with B. So if we take B away, we will mutilate any contents communal with B. Consequently there is no such neat division. (This is why, in the proof of T8, we have to resort to T2.)

The reason for this disparity from classes is that, in the System, we do not have the atomic basis of 'elements' (members of classes). Such an atomic basis presupposes that simple difference rather than *containing* is the basic notion. Now an atomic basis affords maximum divisibility, and for this reason is convenient for analysis. But regarded as a feature of reality, it remains an hypothesis, and has no place in the System, which purports to be a logical system. Moreover, the notion of simple difference is clear only because negative, and its negativity is possible only by applying negation to the positive notion of community, as in Abbreviation 2. Therefore simple difference presupposes community. And since community in turn pre-supposes *containing*, simple difference also presupposes *containing*, and *containing* is logically prior to simple difference. This is why it is absurd to think of a content in the extensional (atomic) way, as dividing between this content and the residual content of the term.

If *containing* is not to be conceived extensionally, it is natural to look for an intensional way of conceiving it. But intensionality depends upon logical form and hence upon identity. The intensionality of *containing* is thus shown by A4, which directly connects *containing* with identity. Two other forms of A4 can be obtained by applying A2, *viz.* (1) If each of two terms contains the other, they are identical, and (2) If neither of two terms is discrepant from the other, they are identical. The first of these connects *containing* even more firmly with identity. Again, it is very easy to prove, in the System, that any term contains itself (T1). Here, *containing* necessarily has identity as a special case. By contrast, in the theory of classes, the corresponding relation of inclusion does not necessarily have identity as a special case; it is simply that logicians find it convenient to define inclusion as covering the special case of identity. (Or are they, perhaps,

driven by a hidden logical compulsion to do so?) In any case
it is clear that *containing* must, from every point of view, be
counted as intensional in character.

4. *Continuity*. A3, D1

Content and continuity are the basic notions of the System.
Content has reference to a special sort of relation, continuity is
an aspect of relation in general.

In *A Dictionary of Philosophy* (Pan), a relation is defined as 'a
propositional function of two or more arguments'. What this
means in ordinary language is that a relation is anything
assertable in one sentence about two or more things. For
example, if I say 'A is round and B is healthy', or 'A is different
in nature from B', or 'A is not connected with B', or 'A is
unrelated to B', I am in each case said to be asserting the
existence of a relation between A and B.

This is the meaning of 'relation' used in modern logic, and
I shall call it the 'abstract' meaning. I chose the four examples
to show that the abstract meaning is in conflict with the
ordinary meaning. In each case we want to ask, How can *this*
relate two terms? This brings out the fact that our ordinary
standard for what constitutes a relation demands some *connection* between the terms. Thus, of three meanings of 'relation'
given in Peter A. Angeles' *A Dictionary of Philosophy*, the first
meaning is 'connection'.

There is one respect in which the abstract meaning of
'relation' is supported by ordinary language. We can say, of
many different pairs of terms, that one of the two terms is
longer than the other, and correspondingly in formal logic that
one has the relation R to the other. In line with this it is
ordinarily acceptable to say, '*Longer than* is a relation'. Here, the
meaning of 'relation' is implied to be general, in suchwise as to
exclude its being particular, *i.e.* it is implied to be abstract.
A relation (with this meaning) is implied to be always one and
the same abstract thing, regardless of what the particular case
is, and indeed regardless of whether there are any particular
cases. There being a certain relation does not (with this
meaning) imply that it has terms.

This divorce between the abstract relation and the concrete situation of terms in particular relationship, results in an unsolvable problem about how the relation is to 'apply' to its terms, *i.e.* relate to its terms. This would seem to raise a difficulty about the truth of A3. But the difficulty has its source not in A3, but in the treatment of a relation as abstract. For if a relation does indeed relate two terms, then *it* must relate them, *i.e.* it must include any 'additional' relations which are required for completing the relation. This consideration points to the need to treat a relation not only as connecting its terms but as being on the same level as its terms, *i.e.* as not abstract but particularised along with its terms. Accordingly, for the System, we conceive a relation not only as a connection but as particular. And this, too, accords with the ordinary meaning, for we can say not only '*Longer than* is a relation', but also 'Any case of *longer than* is a relation'.

But in reasoning (in the System) we must, to avoid equivocation, keep to one meaning of 'relation'. Therefore in accepting the concrete (particular) meaning we reject the abstract meaning. This does not imply, however, that in being particular a relation is not of a general kind. The *validity* of reasoning about relations does depend upon there being kinds of relation. For example, the proof of T5, *viz.* that two directly related terms are communal, must obviously depend upon finding a necessary connection between the kinds of relation expressed by the words 'direct' and 'communal'. At the same time, the *possibility* of reasoning about relations depends upon conceiving the relevant kinds of relation as exemplified together in one particular relation. For it is only in the particular case that any logical connection between the kinds is made manifest. Therefore I repeat that throughout the System I am basically operating with relations as particular (though also possessed of general features). In this I do not depart from the practice in logic of reasoning explicitly in terms of variables rather than in terms of abstract kinds.

Although I have argued that the meaning of 'relation' which I have adopted accords with the ordinary meaning (when ambiguity in the latter is removed), the validity of the System as a logical system does not depend upon this. But accordance with the ordinary meaning is relevant to the truth of premisses of proofs for some later theorems (T13 and T14), where special relations such as knowing are involved.

These preliminaries were to ensure that nothing stands in the way of treating every relation as implying connectedness *and hence unity* of the related terms. This brings us to the main task of the chapter, which is to clarify the relevant notion of unity. ('Continuity' is the word by which I shall subsequently designate the clarified form of unity.)

Normally we think of terms as related only when they are first understood to be different. Moreover, in order to prove the Relation Theorem adequately, we have to begin by accommodating those who believe that it is possible for simply different terms to be related. Now if terms are different, this is naturally assumed to exclude their identity, and in the case of simple difference the exclusion of all identity is quite explicit. But a relation between different terms still implies unity. Therefore the form of unity implied would have to be a form other than identity. The first step towards the notion of continuity is to conceive (as best we can) a form of unity covering indeed identity, but more particularly extending to such unity as lies beyond identity.

How are we to conceive the relevant form of unity other than identity? The most obvious step is to think in terms of system rather than relation. In a system, the terms are understood to exist simultaneously, as if within a single view. It is as if we conceived the unity of the terms by enclosing them in a ring. The terms are in themselves different, so we apply an enclosure from outside to unite them. An enclosure is external to the system, *i.e.* it is a form of unity external to the terms considered as a plurality. Its function is to divide what is within the enclosure from what is outside. In doing so it introduces no relation between the enclosure itself and the terms enclosed. Of course, a division would normally arise when a region (or 'medium') of one kind is juxtaposed to a region of another kind. If we conceive a real medium as within the enclosure (and presumably another as outside), then we can at once conceive each term as related through the medium to the enclosure, and thence through the enclosure to one another. Otherwise not. Thus the enclosure unites the terms only if there is a medium within the enclosure to supply the principle of unity. But if we already have this medium, it will relate and unite the terms directly, *i.e.* independently of the enclosure. The enclosure is redundant.

As with enclosure, so with any form of unity external to the system. For example, the external medium would be an external unity; and it would fail by itself to unite the terms, just as the enclosure by itself fails. In failing to unite, an external unity draws attention to an internal medium as the genuinely uniting factor. The true unity is an internal unity, *i.e.* a form of unity internal to the system of the related terms.

The expression 'internal unity' must not be confused with the expression 'internal relation'. Internal unity is internal to the *system* of the related terms, but an internal relation is internal to the *terms* themselves. The contrast is further accentuated by the fact that, in internal unity, it is just the aspect of unity other than identity that has to be taken account of in proofs, and this corresponds to external rather than to internal relation. On the whole, it is fortunate that we shall, at a later stage, be able to use the more descriptive word 'continuity' in place of the expression 'internal unity'.

An important conclusion of Part I is that there can be *no* form of unity other than identity (see T9 Cor.). In view of this, I believe it is impossible in the end to make the conception of such a form of unity transparently clear. We have to fall back on the ordinary vague notion of an external relation. If we begin by thinking of the relation as direct although external (*i.e.* as semi direct), we have nevertheless to think of it as extended between the terms, since we are taking the terms to be simply different. But this spatialisation of the relation must carry with it the idea that the relation is capable of division into parts. But how is a relation divisible into parts? Only by being separated into many relations, each linked to the next by a common term. This brings us to the notion of an indirect relation, in which there may be any number of intermediate terms, linked together in a series to form a chain of relations and terms. It is here that A3 has its typical application. A3 claims that if even a single link is missing from the chain, the alleged relation between the terms is non-existent. A relation, to relate its terms, must be complete. Completeness is a relevant notion only if the relation has several parts or links. And completeness becomes *continuity* when the number of links is conceived as being as great as we please. It is in such circumstances that A3 is applied in the proof of T6.

Let us recapitulate. We have clarified the notion of unity-other-than-identity, firstly by eliminating external unity as spurious, secondly by showing that the relevant internal unity must be conceived on the model of external relation, and thence on the model of a chain of relations whose number can be indefinitely increased. At this point the word 'continuity' becomes appropriate.

This is a reduction of unity other than identity to continuity. It implies that *all* unity other than identity reduces to continuity. But next we extend the meaning of the word 'continuity' to include not only unity other than identity, but also identity itself. For there is certainly no discontinuity in the passage from a term to itself. The consequence is that continuity now includes *all* unity.

If the notion of a system suggests a spatial view of unity (as a simultaneous togetherness of terms), the notion of continuity implies a temporal view of unity. Such a view of unity is in any case inseparable from the idea of a relation, for it is a familiar truth that a relation has two senses,[1] *i.e.* directions. The reason for this is that, given two terms A and B, we can 'go' or 'pass' either from A to B or from B to A. Any direction has its opposite direction; any kind of relation has its converse kind of relation. And in general the converse kind of relation is different, *e.g.* *shorter than* is different from *longer than*. The notion of *passing* from one term to another is thus a logically necessary adjunct to conceiving the terms as related.

However, both in A3 and for the general notion of relation itself as directional, the word 'pass' introduces tacit reference to an observer, whose attention is conceived as passing from the one term to the other. In A3 the hypothetical observer has to ensure that there is no gap of unrelatedness at any point in the path from one term to the other. Since A3 presupposes an observer, it could well be inferred that the personal identity of the observer is also presupposed, and hence that in A3 we have

[1] Bertrand Russell, *Principles of Mathematics*, 2nd ed., § 94. (At this early stage of modern logic, a relation was still understood as a connection.)

already tacitly reduced continuity to identity, thus begging the whole issue (see T9 Cor.). But firstly, if indeed there is such a presupposition, it is, as I have already shown, a result of the logically necessary introduction of the notion of *passing* from one term to the other; and so it is proved rather than assumed that all continuity is identity. Secondly, in the proofs I have avoided using any assumption of the personal identity of the observer. A3 is used only objectively. For both reasons there is no real begging of the question.

Now let us look at D1. The condition of continuity, which in A3 is claimed to hold axiomatically for any relation, is in D1 used to define what a term is. (Hence T4, which says that any relation is a term.) However, D1 defines the word 'a' (meaning 'one') in 'a term', rather than the word 'term' itself, leaving it completely open what a term is in its content, apart from its form of unity. But we have found that all unity is continuity. Therefore in stipulating that a term must be continuously one, we allow it to have *any* real unity. This makes D1 so unrestricted in its scope as to include any existing thing whatsoever, and provides for a correspondingly unrestricted application of proofs (see especially T12 and T13).

Since continuity is the only real form of unity, in the absence of continuity there is no unity at all. This gives the force of the word 'unrelated' in A3 and D1. If continuity is broken by any unrelatedness, then there is no unity at all left, not even of the weakest kind. There could no longer be *one* term (see the test as used in T2 and T8). The situation is much the same in the ordinary use of the word 'relation'. For the word comes to be applied to any specific connection which, on account of the difference between the terms connected, is denied to be identity. Relation would thus be denied only when no connection at all, even of the weakest sort, is discoverable between the terms.

In this chapter we have concentrated upon the first part of A3, which has very important applications in T6 and T5. But the second part is also used in the proofs, *e.g.* in T2 and T3. One simple form of it is that if two terms are each related to a third they are related to one another.

Because the notion of unity as it stands is too vague for use in proofs, we had to clarify it by casting out false forms of unity and refining what was left. But 'continuity' is a technical word, and the philosophical significance of a statement containing it may not be apparent. In that case we can translate it back again into ordinary language, replacing the word 'continuity' by the word 'unity', in virtue of the conclusion that all unity is continuity (and vice versa, obviously). For example, although the philosophical significance of T9 Cor. may not be apparent, there is no doubt about the philosophical significance of the statement that all *unity* is identity.

5. *Terms and Relations in General.* T1-T4

The purpose of T1-T4 is to pave the way for the subsequent theorems T5-T9. T1-T4 are mixed in character and general in their treatment of relations, whereas T5-T9 form a single development in one direction, as well as being more specialised in their treatment of relations.

T.1 *Any term contains itself.* (A2)
    Proof. A term not contained in itself would be discrepant from itself (by A2), and hence not identical with itself, which is absurd.

Comment

This simple theorem is used in the proof of T3. Apart from its purely formal use, it is of importance because it throws light upon the nature of a term and upon the nature of *containing*. The development of the System in Part II will show increasingly that a term can only be interpreted as a form of consciousness. But if so, then a content of a term can only be interpreted as a state of consciousness or an object of consciousness, and *containing* becomes the kind of relation which occurs between consciousness and its object (for presumably a state of consciousness is always accessible as an object to the consciousness in that state). What the theorem says, on this interpretation, is that any form of consciousness is, potentially at least, a form of *self*-consciousness.

Apart from this interpretation, the theorem implies that *containing* has to have identity as a special case. This anticipates

T8, which implies that *containing* has to *be* identity. Moreover, because T1 is a significant theorem (unlike its counterpart in elementary theory of sets, which is more like a definition), it supports a non-extensional interpretation of *containing*. This accords with what was said at the end of ch. 3.

T1 also suggests that identity is not trivial, but provides for a difference between the terms identified; and this again is borne out by the later development of the System.

T2. *Any two terms of a system are related in the system.* (A3, D1, D2)

Proof. Suppose there are two terms A and B in a system S, which are unrelated in S.

We distinguish in S between an A-group of terms consisting of A and every term in S related in S to A, and a B-group consisting of B and every term in S related in S to B.

If any member of the A-group were identical with, or related to, any member of the B-group, there would be a continuity of relationship from A to B through the relevant members of the groups. Hence, by A3, A would be related in S to B, which contradicts the original supposition. Therefore no member of the A-group is related in S to any member of the B-group.

Any remaining terms in S would have to be unrelated in S to any member of either group.

The conclusion is that each of the two groups is a content (or contents) of S unrelated in S to the remaining content(s) of S. Hence D1 is contradicted and S is not a term, and therefore by D2 not a system. Hence the supposition is contradictory and the theorem is true.

Cor. Any two contents of a term are related in the term.

Comment

A3 can be used as a test of the presence of relationship. D1 can similarly be used to test whether a given complex can form a single term. They are both continuity tests, and they are continuity tests at the same level of strength. What they both say is that something purporting to be a system cannot be a system if it is divided completely, *i.e.* right through, by a gap (or gaps) of unrelatedness.

Now it is one thing to say that there is such a gap right through the given complex, but quite another to say that there is a gap of unrelatedness merely between two terms of the complex. This is made obvious if we imagine a complex involving a large number of terms, related in various ways and not simply as a series. What T2 proves is that a gap between two terms implies a gap right through. So T2 is a much stronger (more powerful) test of relationship than the other two. It is used as this strong test in T3 and in T8.

T2 can also be used to supplement D2. It tells us that a system contains not only two terms but also at least one relation between any two terms.

T3. *Two communal terms are directly related.* (T1, A3, D2, T2, D4)

Proof. Let A be any term, and let B be any content of A other than A itself.

A is a content of A, by T1; but A is also related to A, by A3. Therefore this content of A, *viz.* A, is related to A.

A has at least two contents, *viz.* A and B. Hence by D2, A is a system. But by T2, the two terms A and B of this system are related (in the system). Thus not only is A related to A, but B is related to A. And since B is *any* content of A other than A, it follows that any content of A, unconditionally, is related to A. Hence any case of *containing* is a relation.

Now in any case of community, we have an unbroken series of two *containing* relations. So it follows by A3 that any case of community is a relation, *i.e.* two communal terms are related.

Moreover, if two terms are communal, *i.e.* have at least one content numerically the same, this is ensured solely by what the contents of the terms are. Hence by D4 any relation of community is direct, *i.e.* two communal terms are directly related.

Cor. 1. If one term contains another, the two are related.

Cor. 2. Two communal terms are related.

Cor. 3. Two communal terms are in fully direct relation (see case 3 under D4).

Comments

Of the four propositions, T3 itself and the three corollaries, T3 was chosen as the main theorem because it is the converse of T5. But the main part of the proof of T3 consists in proving that *containing* and community are kinds of relation (Cor. 1 and 2). These are the important results here. Anything subsequently proved about relations in general will therefore automatically apply to relations of these two kinds.

The transposition of T3 Cor. 3 is that terms not in any fully direct relation are simply different. We must be careful not to read this as meaning that terms in a non-fully direct relation (*i.e.* in a semi direct or an indirect relation) are simply different. For two terms would, in general, be in relations of more than one kind (such as distance apart, relative size, etc.). Consequently terms in a non-fully direct relation are not debarred from being in a fully direct relation too.

T4. *Any relation is a term.* (A3, D1)

Proof. By A3, in passing from one term of a relation to the other, via the relation, we reach no point at which what is so far traversed is unrelated to what is yet to be traversed. Any relation therefore satisfies the condition of continuous unity laid down in D1, and so is a term.

Comments

In the next chapter we begin to speak of relations as contained or not contained in their terms. If relations were thought to differ in type from their terms, this would not make sense. The supposition of a difference in type was removed, I hope, in ch. 4, where it was pointed out that, in the System, we conceive relations as particular, on the same level as their terms. In view of this, T4 should not come as a surprise. T4 proves the congruity of term and relation, and the legitimacy of speaking of the latter as contained in the former.

The theorem should not be taken as reducing relations to terms. For A3 is a *truth* about relation, leaving 'relation' undefined; whereas D1 is merely a *definition* of 'term', defining it moreover by reference to relation. So T4 is to be viewed, along with D1, as indicating that *term* is a secondary notion modelled upon the basic notion of *relation*.

6. Direct Relations. T5

T5. *Two directly related terms are communal.* (A1, A3, D3, D4)

Proof. Suppose that R is any relation between any two simply different terms A and B.

Because A and B have nothing in common, there is no content of A at which we have already passed to B. Consequently, to pass from A to B, we have to leave A at some content C of A, in order to reach B at some content D of B.

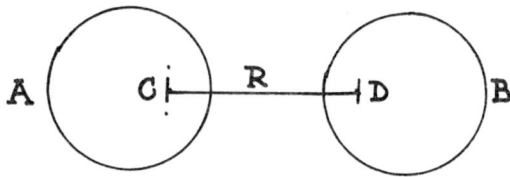

Now if C and D had something in common, A and B would, by A1, have that same thing in common, which contradicts the supposition that A and B are simply different. So C and D are simply different. Thus for continuity between A and B, there has to be a *change* from C (where we leave A) to the simply different term D (where we reach B). And by A3, any relation R between A and B must be continuous, and hence contain such a change.

No change occurs either *at* C or *at* D. Therefore the change from C to D must occur after we leave A and before we reach B, *i.e.* in an interval of the passage in which no content either of A or of B is present. Accordingly the change is simply different both from A and from B. Thus R has a content simply different from A and from B, and so by D3 is an indirect relation.

But R is any relation between any two simply different terms. Thus any relation between two simply different terms is indirect. By transposition, if a relation between two terms is direct (and hence by D4 not indirect), then the terms cannot be simply different, and must therefore be communal. That is, two directly related terms must be communal.

Cor. Semi direct relations are impossible. (See note on D4. A semi direct relation is a direct relation whose terms are not implied to be communal.)

Comments

To guard against possible misunderstanding, I mention at this point that I regard valid formal proof as final, and that comments are accordingly not aimed at supplementing formal proof by informal proof, but *e.g.* at relating the theorems to experience.

1. The diagrammatic representation of terms in relation suggests that a semi direct relation is represented when the diagrams for the terms are drawn as touching. Similarly the touching of geometrical figures appears to *be* a semi direct

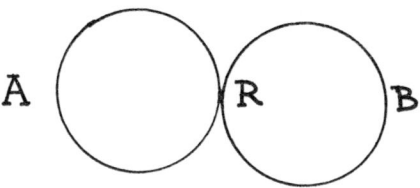

relation between the figures. For nothing external to the terms seems to be needed in order to relate them, and on the other hand there appears to be nothing in common. But mathematical analysis does not bear this out. Touching is normally defined in terms of community: two figures touch when the area in common is made indefinitely small. This means that the common area can be made as small as we please, not that it can ever cease to exist. If, on the other hand, touching is defined in terms of the mutual approach of the figures, the mutual externality of the figures is presupposed and always preserved, and their relation is always implied to be indirect.

2. Historically the crucial example of an apparently semi direct relation is resemblance. On the one hand it is not an indirect relation, because only the two terms themselves are needed to ensure that they do resemble one another in just this way. On the other hand, resemblance has widely been assumed, since Hume's time, not to involve identity (as community), and hence not to be a fully direct relation. For resemblance admits of degrees, and this appears to by-pass the need of any point of exact identity. Moreover, there appear to be simple terms, such as the colours blue and green, which, although resembling one another (more, *e.g.*, than blue and scarlet), defy all efforts to analyse out any respect of identity which would explain their resemblance.[1] Nominalists have made use of this experiential

[1] See Richard I. Aaron, *The Theory of Universals*, 2nd ed., Oxford, 1967, pp. 72-5.

situation to replace universals by particular relations of resemblance.

Is it strictly the case that the resemblance between two terms does not imply their community? Resemblance occurs within our experience when we perceive two terms, compare them, and find them to be alike. Perceptual comparison between two terms is the model upon which we conceive the relevant system. Two terms resemble one another in fact so long as they form a system of the relevant kind, *i.e.* so long as the terms belong to an actual situation characterised by the kind of likeness which would be seen between the terms if we could perceive and compare them. Their likeness in the situation connects the terms in one system, just as a comparison within perception connects two terms in one view.

Consider the colour resemblance between two surfaces, one mid-blue and the other mid-green. Resemblance can be close or remote, varying by degrees between. This implies the need of a scale of all the shades between mid-blue and mid-green if we are to say that they resemble one another. Between any two successive shades there is a maximum resemblance, so that any greater resemblance than this would be identity (of shade).

Suppose that the two given shades are A and H, and the scale between them B,C ... G. Our 'system', within which relationship between A and H occurs, is the whole scale, *viz.* A,B,C ... G,H. Because the relation is direct, the relation and

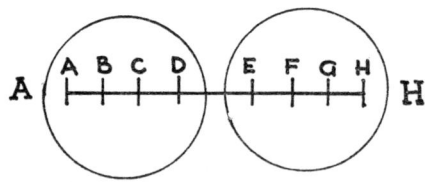

hence the system is internal to the terms. Let us suppose, then, that the part A,B,C,D of the system is in A, and the part E,F,G,H in H. (This follows case 2 under D4.) Does this ensure that no part of the system remains external to the terms? No. For an essential part of the system is the maximum resemblance between D and E, which so far is contained in neither term. For the relation to be complete, either A must contain E, or H must contain D. In either case the obvious result is that the terms are now communal.

The conclusion is that resembling terms *are* communal, but not in the straightforward way. The historical difficulties have arisen partly because it has been assumed that what would have to be in common between the terms, if anything is in common, would be something simple relative to the terms. We have seen, however, that what must be in common contains at least two terms co-ordinate with the given terms, and possibly the whole scale of terms containing the given terms. (This corresponds to case 3 under D4.) Moreover, the fact that remote resemblances and contrasts occur suggests that each member of the scale contains the whole scale potentially, and not just a part. The part between two members is then actualised in both of them when they are compared, depending of course upon the clarity of the comparison. Thus not only does the scale contain each member of it, but each member contains the scale, and any member contains every other member (cp. T8).

The way in which community is here implied is traditionally associated not with theories about the relation of resemblance, but with Hegelian theories of opposites. It should be remembered that Hume classified contrariety along with resemblance as an internal relation.[1] And this is surely correct, for once the particular terms are given (*e.g.* a sensation of heat and a sensation of coldness), the relation is fixed. However, it is even harder to admit that opposites contain one another than to admit that similars contain one another. But the above reasoning about resemblance applies in a modified way to typical relations of opposition. For, granting that a relation of opposition is internal, it can be complete only on condition that it exists, with its terms, in at least one of its terms; and presumably (by symmetry) in the other too. Even opposites are, in a special way, communal. Careful examination of examples reveals that in no case can we find a relation which is truly semi direct.

[1] David Hume, *A Treatise of Human Nature*, London, 1911, Bk. I, Pt. III, section 1, p. 74.

7. *Indirect Relations.* T6, T7

An intermediate term C for an indirect relation between two terms A and B is that content of the relation which ensures the indirectness (or externality) of the relation. Thus the intermediate term C is the term specified in D3 as simply different from the terms A and B of the relation. Therefore by T5 transposed, the relations of C to A and to B must be indirect, so that these two relations in turn require intermediate terms, each by T5 transposed introducing two more indirect relations, and so on to infinity. This in principle is Bradley's argument against external relations.[1] But, critics ask, why should the series *not* be infinite? The proof of T6 begins by showing why not.[2]

T6. *Indirect relations are impossible.* (A3, T5, D3)

Proof. Between the two terms of an indirect relation, there is a series S of one or more intermediate terms with their relations. Between any two terms of S, a further term X of S is needed if and only if it is needed as an intermediate term for the relation between them, *i.e.* if and only if, without X, there is no relation between them. Therefore if, however many terms of S are introduced in this way, a further term is always needed, there always remain two terms of S with no relation between them; so the series always remains broken by a gap of unrelatedness, and A3 is always contradicted. In the end, therefore, each intermediate term in S must be related, on each side of itself, to a 'neighbour', between which and itself no further term is needed. There is consequently no infinite regress. Since the relation between two neighbours (in this final series) requires no intermediate term, it is direct, and by T5 neighbours are therefore communal. Hence, in an indirect relation, each intermediate term has two neighbours which are communal with it. This we call 'the neighbourhood condition'.

On the other hand: In the last stage of the construction of S,

---

[1] F. H. Bradley, *Appearance and Reality*, 2nd ed., London, 1920, p. 21.

[2] But a former version of the proof of T6 failed to show why not. I am grateful to Dr Neil Tennant for pointing this out at a Department Discussion Group meeting at Edinburgh University, May 1981.

each new member of S introduced is introduced as an intermediate term to relate the two terms which become its neighbours. By D3, such a new member is therefore simply different
from each of its neighbours. This we call 'the externality
condition' for indirect relations. It plainly contradicts the
neighbourhood condition. Hence indirect relations, which
require both conditions, are impossible.

The two conditions are mutually contradictory in a less
obvious way. Whereas the neighbourhood condition demands
a definite halt at some point in the proliferation of members of
S, the externality condition demands proliferation at every
point reached, thus implying an infinite regress.

T7. *Two related terms are communal.* (T5, T6)
   Proof. This follows at once from T5 and T6.

Comments
   Since external relations are impossible, how is it that in
spatial relations we seem so obviously to have actual cases of
external relation? For practical purposes, the distance of two
things apart is determinable independently of the constitutions
of the things. But in the scientific context this is not so. For
gravitational and electro-magnetic fields are properties of
physical things which affect their distance apart, and conversely the distance of two things apart at any moment affects
the state of the field between them. The impression that
relations of distance are external is due to our inability in
practice to detect the relevant variations of these fields. But we
have only to observe some simple phenomenon of magnetism
or static electricity to realise that the distance apart of two
things can modify a power in the things to attract or repel. The
things react to the distance, and to do this they must in some
way 'take up' the distance into themselves.

   This 'taking up' of a condition into a thing seems to be the
only feasible explanation of the relation of cause and effect.
Whitehead calls it 'prehension'.[1] The reason why it does give a
genuine explanation is that it is modelled upon the way in
which consciousness can be observed to operate in ourselves.
In terms of consciousness, there is an obvious way in which

[1] A. N. Whitehead, *Process and Reality*, London, 1929, Pt. I, ch. 1, § 2.

distances are internal to a human being. He prehends distances systematically, forming a map of his spatial environment in his subconscious mind. By its means he is able, say, to visit someone living at a distance from him. And in the course of the journey, his map is being steadily modified by his prehensions of the changing distances.

Following the last comment on T4 (ch. 5), the internality of relations is not to be viewed as reducing relations to their terms, but as a step in the reduction of the manyness of terms to an underlying unity of relatedness. As a consequence, the pluralism which would result from accepting terms as ultimates gives place to a conception of reality distinctly favourable to monism.

8. *Relation and Identity*. T8, T9

T8. *Two communal terms are identical.* (A2, A1, T7, T2, A4)

Proof. Let A and B be two terms having a content C in common.

Suppose that one of the terms, say A, is not contained in the other, B. Then by A2, A has some content D simply different from B.

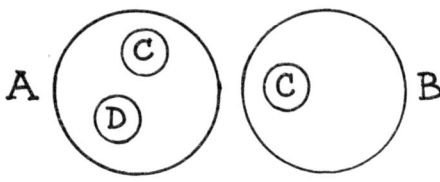

Since C is contained in B, if any content of D were contained in C, then by A1 it would be contained in B, which contradicts the simple difference between D and B. Hence D is simply different from C as well as from B. That is, the two contents C and D of A are simply different, and hence by T7 transposed are unrelated. But since A is a system containing the terms C and D, C and D must be related (by T2). The supposition is therefore contradictory, and each of the terms must be contained in the other. Consequently either term contains the other and is contained in the other. Thus by A2 (transposition of second part) either term contains the other without being discrepant from it, and so by A4 each is identical with the other.

Cor. All continuity is identity.

T9. *Two related terms are identical.* (T7, T8)
    Proof. At once from T7 and T8.

Comments

Although these two theorems follow straightforwardly from the Relation Theorem (T7), they are far more difficult to accept, since they seem to leave no room for the existence of real differences between objects. For between any two objects of experience we can always find some relation, and hence by T9 prove identity. This would normally be taken to exclude difference between them.

A common response of idealists to this kind of difficulty has been to maintain that all difference is illusory. But an illusion of difference would be a real difference in perception, with no real difference corresponding to it in the object perceived. This presupposes that there are real differences in perception, and further that there is a real difference between the illusory perception and its object. Consequently illusions of difference provide no escape from real differences; and as we saw above, real differences between objects are accompanied by relationship between them, and hence by their identity (T9). This necessitates difference-in-identity.

The problem, then, is to understand how difference can be compatible with identity. But before offering a solution, I want to stress the urgency of the problem, by showing how problems repeatedly arise in philosophy, as a result of failure to solve it, *i.e.* as a result of the belief that difference is always incompatible with identity. In this account of these problems, I shall use the word 'division' or the word 'separation' for difference incompatible with identity. One immediate effect will be to show that the proof of T8 is not a series of formal devices which fortunately bring about the required result, but represents a pervasive though subconscious trend in philosophical thought.

Consider first the problem about the relation between universal and particular. A universal is definable as something capable of being common to different particulars, *e.g.* different particular spots on a dress could all be of the same shade of green. Now particulars are always assumed to be not only different but separate from one another. Each particular, then, comes to be credited not only with a component which it has in common with the others, but also with a component peculiar to itself, not possessed by the others. As in the proof of T8, there is now a division *within* the particular, at least as strong as the separation *between* particulars. Accordingly the particular has to be identified with one or other only of its components, since otherwise it would be two things instead of one. But the differences between particulars are more obvious to the senses than their common qualities; so each particular becomes identified with its differentiating component, and the universal (*i.e.* the common component) is extrapolated, becoming 'abstract'. This obviously contradicts the way in which a universal is defined. Moreover no solution is to be found in nominalism. For the evidences for universals can then be met only by introducing relations of resemblance between particulars, and relation returns us to community (T7). The only way to avert paradox is to conceive a universal not as abstract but as 'concrete', *i.e.* as not only common to its particularised instances, but as identical with each of them in spite of their differences.

Just as a universal may have many instances, so a thing may have many qualities. As a result similar problems arise about the thing-quality relation. Because qualities are assumed to be not only different but separate from one another, a separation arises between thing and quality. The quality is identified with the component of itself which differentiates it from the other qualities, leaving the thing itself as a residual core denuded of all qualities. The solution is to conceive the one thing as in each of its qualities in spite of their differences.

An examination of reflexive paradoxes would take us too deeply into logical technicalities. In my opinion the solution is, as before, to replace the assumed basis of separation (*e.g.* between the members of a class) by difference-in-identity.

Let us return to the main question, expressing it in a somewhat different form. We ordinarily believe that if two terms are identical, this negates their difference; can we see how it is possible for identity *not* to negate difference? To this I shall answer that we *can* see how this is possible, provided we make appropriate revisions in our normally accepted views (1) of the nature of external existence, (2) of the way in which negation operates in thought and in external existence.

At least in an assertion of identity, difference is not only possible but necessary. For we need two ways of referring to objects of a certain sort, if we are to assert that there is just one object, and not two, singled out (by the mechanism of reference). But we seem to escape from this difference as soon as we consider what it is that makes the assertion true. For the condition of truth seems obviously to be that there should be just *one* object. Thus the ordinary concept of identity appears to be based upon the ordinary experience of unity in a perceived object.

If this ordinary view were intended as a general claim to the effect that we conceive identity in terms of unity, it would certainly fail. For we found in ch. 4 that all unity is continuity, and T9 Cor. now adds that all continuity is identity, the obvious conclusion being that all unity is identity. Thus we cannot in general explain identity in terms of unity. All that could be hoped for is to regard the reduction of unity to identity as purely conceptual, and still accept the word 'unity' as the most appropriate description of the fact which makes an assertion of identity true.

We now ask whether the implication of difference (present in assertions of identity) can be avoided (a) at the level of concepts, (b) at the level of facts. At the conceptual level, the most promising way of avoiding the implication would be to conceive identity as the identity of one thing with itself, rather than as the identity of an object A with an object B. But even so, to identify a thing with itself it is necessary to differentiate between the thing as identified with something, and the (same) thing as the something with which identification occurs. Conceptually at least, identity therefore implies difference.

What about a fact of identity? A fact of identity, whether or not we describe it in terms of unity, is not any fact we please, it is a fact of a certain sort. However, a fact *is* a fact of a certain sort only in so far as *it completely conforms to the concept which defines it as being of that sort.* Moreover we have seen that any concept of unity resolves into some form of the concept of identity; so that identity is the only concept by which a fact of identity can be defined. But we have also seen that a necessary part of the concept of identity is the implication of difference. It follows that the same implication of difference must be present in the fact of identity.

How is it then that a fact of identity (as the unity of a perceived object) seems positively to exclude difference? There is only one way of accounting for this. However perfectly we may suppose the fact to exclude difference, neither it nor our thought of it are ever quite free of difference. Negation therefore must operate here by suppression, not as ideal elimination; and yet at the same time it generates the impression of ideal elimination. The difference between the thought and the fact is a matter of degree. In the fact the suppression is greater, more stable, and more independent of our volition. The result is a one-sided form of difference-in-identity, which we call 'unity', in the belief that no difference at all is present in it.

We are now familiar with the truth, discoverable by inspection, that in order to conceive identity we necessarily conceive a difference between the terms identified. Moreover, at this purely conceptual level, there is no fact of identity standing in the way, to persuade us that the difference is made impossible by the identity. Thus there is no problem about understanding the implication of difference by identity at the conceptual level. My argument has been that a fact of identity must contain at least all that is necessary to the concept (even if it contains more). Therefore the fact contains the implication of difference just as the concept does. Consequently, having seen how the implication is possible in the concept, we have automatically seen how it is possible in the fact. The difficulty arises because negation, in suppressing the difference, produces the impression that the difference has been eliminated, and hence the further impression that difference is not compatible with identity. But suppression is not elimination, and the fact is understood when the thought is understood.

What the System proves is the converse implication, _viz._ that difference implies identity. (Although not quite proved in T9, it is finally proved in T14.) The explanations given of the one implication apply equally to the other. Thus any remaining difficulties about understanding how difference-in-identity is possible should have disappeared.

I would hazard the generalisation that all physical existence is thought developed in a one-sided way, as if involving suppression.

PART II

CONSCIOUSNESS

9. *The Existence of Consciousness.* A5

1. To know that consciousness exists, I need only pay attention to my seeing rather than to the things I see; or to my remembering rather than to my memories; or to any other form of awareness rather than to the particular objects of that awareness. By a slight shift of attention, I can turn away from the objects that usually occupy me, to my awareness of these objects. Having done this, an example of awareness is fully present to me, and I know directly that awareness exists, *i.e.* that consciousness exists.

Direct knowledge such as this I call knowledge by 'intuition', as opposed to knowledge by inference. Intuition is direct knowing of some fact, implicit in direct awareness of the subject-matter which the fact is about. Thus we know by intuition that consciousness exists, because a direct knowing that consciousness exists is implicit in our direct awareness of consciousness, *i.e.* in our self-consciousness. For practical purposes we can therefore take the expressions 'intuition', 'direct knowing', 'direct awareness', and 'direct consciousness' to be interchangeable.

2. It is important to see that all valid proof presupposes intuition, and hence that knowledge by intuition is as sound as knowledge by valid proof. In saying that all valid proof presupposes intuition, I am not referring to the intuition needed for the assurance of the truth of premisses. For at least two forms of argument, *viz.* reductio ad absurdum and proof by supposition, avoid dependence upon premisses. I am referring to the intuition needed to know the truth of the logical principles used in the argument. For example, to see that a reductio ad absurdum argument is valid, one of the truths that we have to know is that a proposition and its contradictory cannot both be true together. This principle is known through

intuition, *viz.* through an intuition of the nature of negation. A pre-formal step of reasoning then occurs from this intuition of the nature of negation to the logical principle (the law of non-contradiction).

It follows that we cannot and need not prove a truth that is basically intuitive, since its being intuitive is as good a justification as any proof can be. Therefore if you dispute what I see to be intuitive, the only conclusion I can draw is that you have not experienced the relevant act of intuition. Consequently all that I can do by way of 'proof' or 'justification' for my intuition, is to focus your attention fully upon it, in the hope that the relevant act of intuition will occur for you as for myself.

3. This, I believe, is what happens in the case of Descartes' 'Cogito' argument for the existence of consciousness: I think, therefore I am.[1] Suppose I doubt, or even deny outright, the proposition that consciousness exists now. Then the doubt or denial is itself an example to me of consciousness existing now, refuting all doubts or denials of it. But of course, I have to take the step of extending the inward experiencing of the act of doubt or denial, to the outward recognition of that act as actually occurring, *i.e.* as existing. It is in this step that the act of intuition unfolds. It is just another case of the shift in attention, described at the outset, from *e.g.* the things I see to my seeing of them. The step is always pre-formal because, like the case of intuiting a logical principle, its starting point is not a proposition but an experience.

An essential aspect of the intuition of consciousness is that it is a true *self*-consciousness, an act of consciousness knowing itself in its own occurrence. It is the kind of self-consciousness explained by Sartre, in his notion of the pre-reflective Cogito.[2] Such true self-consciousness has often been denied by philosophers, because they believe that it belongs to the nature of consciousness that it can be conscious only of what is external to itself, never strictly of itself. An act of consciousness, it is said, can never be aware of its very self, *i.e.* of this present act, but at best of an immediately past act of the same person.

[1] R. Descartes, *Meditations,* in *A Discourse on Method etc.,* London 1912, Meditation 2.

[2] Jean-Paul Sartre, *Being and Nothingness,* New York 1956, Introduction section III.

Stated in the latter form, the criticism takes refuge in our general ignorance of the nature of time. We can by-pass this difficulty by keeping to the simpler but entirely general form of the criticism, *viz.* that an act of being aware can never be aware of this same act. In terms of T9 transposed, there is a short answer to any such contention: if the object of awareness were even discrepant from the awareness of it, it would be unrelated to that awareness, and so awareness of that object would be utterly impossible. Consciousness does indeed habitually represent its object as external to itself (and it is this fact which leads to the fallacious criticism). But consciousness never succeeds in making its object in fact external to itself. So far as the fact is concerned, consciousness always remains related to its object, and hence always identical with its object, never therefore finally losing all *self*-consciousness in its awareness of any object. The unity which consciousness brings to experience is identity, the only possible form of unity (see T9 Cor.). What brings about the unity of experience is the fact that the same consciousness identifies with each of its objects, and the consequence of this fact is that consciousness can always become self-conscious in being conscious of any object.

4. In this post-Rylian era, it is difficult to say a word in favour of Descartes without being accused of dualism.[1] Descartes' dualism rests upon the fact that he claimed to prove not only the existence of consciousness but also the existence of matter. But his proof of the existence of matter (Med. 6) was far more sophisticated than his proof of the existence of consciousness (Med. 2), and altogether different in kind. Having supposed himself (in Med. 3) to have proved that God exists and is not a deceiver, he argued (in Med. 6) that man has a strong natural inclination to believe in the existence of matter, and that since God has given man no means of knowing that matter does not exist, God would be a deceiver if matter in fact did not exist. But *has* God given man no means of knowing that matter does not exist? A relevant means of knowing is proof. So Descartes' argument would collapse as soon as anyone succeeded in finding a satisfactory proof of the non-existence of matter. Soon after Descartes' time, Berkeley claimed to give

[1] See G. Ryle, *The Concept of Mind*, London 1949, ch. 1.

such a proof. I claim to give such a proof in T18 (backed by the System). To be valid, Descartes' proof of the existence of matter would first have to prove the impossibility of proving the non-existence of matter.

5. Having proved at the end of Part I that two *related* terms are identical, it is natural to anticipate the possibility of eventually proving that *any* two terms are identical. We do in fact reach such a proof, *viz.* in T14 Cor. 1. This headlong trend towards identity might suggest that we could take anything whatsoever as the principle of monism, *e.g.* a particular stone found in the garden. Why pick on consciousness?

There are at least three answers to this. The first is that, in order to prove the main theorem of Part II, *viz.* T14, we have to make essential use of the special nature of consciousness. This is what makes T14 stand out as a fundamental, philosophical step in the argument.

The second answer is that, whereas the existence of consciousness can be known directly, the existence of anything else can be known only through its participation in consciousness. In the case of material things (understood to be non-conscious), it is notoriously true that we are directly aware only of qualities which we ascribe to them, not of the things themselves. Can we claim that such qualities exist? But they vary with the conditions of the percipient, and resolve into sensory experiences. I suppose we could pick upon a particular sensory experience, and immortalise it in our existential axiom. But its existence will have gone a moment hence (so far as axiomatic knowledge goes), so as an axiom it would be entirely useless. But consciousness is common to all sensory experiences (and experiences of other kinds), and is the common reason for our knowing that they exist. Although A5 does, indeed, only claim the existence of consciousness now, this is a now which goes on from moment to moment, so long as experience in any form lasts, and certainly so long as there will be anyone to understand the System. There is consequently no chance of A5 becoming relevantly false.

Nevertheless it is a serious drawback in A5, that consciousness can be claimed, axiomatically, only to exist *now* (*i.e.* at least whenever anyone considers the matter), and not necessarily and timelessly. Even the Cogito does not (or at least ought not to) claim the timeless existence of consciousness. Descartes has with justice been criticised for attempting nevertheless to found a system of metaphysics upon the Cogito. Before we can do this, we must first go on to prove the *necessary* existence of consciousness. One of the purposes of Part II of the System is to do just this, and the proof is reached in T17. Now even if the existence of an ordinary thing, quality, or state of affairs were admitted, its necessary existence would be quite another matter. So this incidentally gives us a third reason for picking upon consciousness as the principle of monism.

10. *Extending the Time of Relatedness.* T10, T11

In the proof of the necessary and hence eternal existence of consciousness, there are two outstanding theorems, *viz.* T14 and T16. In T10-T15 we are proving that consciousness exists so long as anything at all exists. This we call the 'semi-eternal' existence of consciousness. Here T14 contributes the essentially new argument. With the further new argument introduced in T16, we are then able, in T17, to infer the unconditionally necessary existence of consciousness.

The purpose of T10 and T11, which occupy us in the present chapter, is to supply a link essential to the proof of T14. In the following two chapters we then begin from another point with T12, going on in natural sequence through T13 to T14, at the end of which we pick up the result of T11 to complete the proof.

The results of these theorems are by no means confined to matters of existence. Perhaps even more important is the aspect of identity.

T10. *A term at any time of its existence is identical with that term at any other time of its existence.* (D1, T9 Cor., T9)

Proof. Here the word 'identical' refers to numerical identity, in accordance with its meaning in the System. Outside the System, we speak of a term as being the 'same' term at successive times, referring only to its continuity (of relationship) from one time to the next. By D1, a term does have to be continuous in time; but it does not, so far, have to remain self-identical. However, it is proved, by T9 Cor., that all continuity *is* identity. So the theorem directly follows. By a reductio argument, using T9 transposed and D1, we can similarly prove:

Cor. 1. No term can gain or lose any content during its existence;

hence *Cor. 2.* Any two terms must be either always communal or always simply different. (For otherwise at least one of the terms would lose or gain a content.)

Comments

1. One reason for the importance of Cor. 1 is that it brings out a philosophical implication of the main theorem T10, *viz.* that all the contents of a term are 'essential' contents, *i.e.* that the term would not be this term if it had more or less than just these contents (properties, etc.). This, indeed, is a paradox. For example, it seems obvious that if you paint a green door red, the door loses its green colour and gains the colour red. But it is no more a paradox than the general paradox of difference-in-identity, of which it is a special case. I offer the following account of it. When a term appears *e.g.* to gain a content, it does not in fact gain that content; rather the status of the content, as content, changes from potentiality to actuality. Thus to say that something is potentially so does not mean that it could be so but is *not* so; it means that it *is* so, but only implicitly, in a way that is not apparent to the level of consciousness which we are then taking as the measure of actuality. The distinction between potential and actual is thus to be understood in terms of remoteness and nearness to the centre of conscious attention, not in terms of the distinction between non-existence and existence.

2. T10 Cor. 2 is a consequence of the essentiality of a term's contents, and is important for its own sake and for T11. By T7

and T3 Cor. 2, relationship and community are equivalent. Therefore T10 Cor. 2 implies that any two terms must be either always related or always unrelated. This amounts to the doctrine of internal relations, with its implication of necessity: there are no external relations (cp. T6), *i.e.* there are no relations which can exist at one time but not at another between the *same* two terms.

The necessity implied by the doctrine becomes more apparent if we interpret T10 Cor. 2 in the following way: Two terms cannot gain or lose community, for then at least one of the terms would gain or lose the common content, and so cease to be itself. Even without T10, there is a certain plausibility about this. Why can we paint a door and a table the same colour, though not a door and a musical note? Presumably it is because a door and a table *already have sufficient in common* to enable us to do this, whereas a door and a musical note have not. The nearer we approach to simple difference, the harder it is to introduce anything 'contingently' in common.

3. Having seen how T10 Cor. 2 bears upon relationship, let us now see how it bears upon identity. It can be expressed by saying that if it is ever true that two terms are communal, then it is necessarily true that they are communal. Statements of community are necessary statements (necessarily true or necessarily false). For otherwise at least one of the terms might not remain itself. Since identity is a special case of community, the same must hold for identity. Statements of identity are necessary statements, for otherwise at least one of the terms identified might not remain itself.

But whereas T10 is required to prove that statements of community are necessary statements, it is easily shown (below) that T10 is not required to prove that identity statements are necessary statements. If we are ever able to judge that A and B are identical, it is because we find that each possesses certain special properties needed to identify it, and because the properties turn out to be the same for each. These are the so-called 'essential' properties. A and B are identical if and only if their essential properties are the same. A change from their identity to their non-identity or vice-versa would accordingly imply a loss or gain by one of them of at least one of its essential properties, *i.e.* it would no longer *be* the thing it was. Such a change is therefore impossible. A true statement of identity is necessarily true.

Because no proposition equivalent to T10 is appealed to in this argument, it is independent of the doctrine of internal relations, and independent of idealism. For this reason Kripke has been able to uphold the necessity of statements of identity by arguments appealing to philosophers of all persuasions.[1]

T.11 *Two terms which can be related must co-exist, and be identical throughout their existence.* (T7, T10, T8)

Proof. To say that two terms 'coexist' is understood to mean that, at any time at which either one exists, the other also exists.

By T7, given two terms A and B which can be related, they can be communal, *i.e.* there is a time at which they can be communal, *i.e.* at which they both exist and are not simply different. (For simple difference would make community *impossible*, as is indicated by T10 Cor. 2.) It follows that A and B *are* communal at this time.

By T8, it now follows that the terms are identical at this time, and by T10 that they are therefore identical at every time of the existence of either term. More precisely, at every time of the existence of, say A, A is identical with B at any time of B's existence. A, at any time of its existence, *is* B. The existence of B is therefore preserved by A at every time of A's existence (and vice-versa by a parallel argument). Consequently the terms coexist, as well as being identical throughout their existence.

Cor. Two terms which can (ever) be related must be related at all times of their existence.

Comments

1. If we omit the first step in the proof of T11, we prove the following weakened form of the theorem: Two terms related at any time of their existence must coexist, and be identical throughout their existence. A correspondingly weakened form of the corollary follows, which extends the time of relatedness from a particular time to all times of the existence of the terms.

The purpose of T11 is to complete the proof of T14. When we come to this proof of T14, it will appear that the weakened

[1] S. A. Kripke, *Naming and Necessity*, 2nd ed., Oxford, 1980.

form of T11 is sufficient. But it is not, and this is why the strong form is proved above. The point will be cleared up in the comments on T14, which will also explain the historical importance of the corollary.

2. The reason why the corollary is not proved directly is that the situation is confused so long as we do not know that the terms coexist, and to prove coexistence we have first to prove identity.

11. *The Unity of Consciousness.* T12, T13

T12. *Any one existence is one term.* (D1)

Proof. This theorem amounts to a decision to use the word 'one' in 'one existence' in the same sense as the word 'one' in 'one term', *viz.* in accordance with the test of continuity laid down in D1.

Comments

We pointed out in ch. 4 that there is no unity by enclosure, and that as a result continuity includes the weakest form of unity, and is therefore implied to be present whenever any form of unity is present. So it is not question-begging to use continuity as a test for unity in general. We naturally use the words 'a' and 'an', along with 'one', in accordance with the continuity test.

The point of T12 is that it enables us to apply theorems about terms to existence. For it ensures that any existence is a special case of a term. The first application is in the following theorem.

T13. *Consciousness is one existing term.* (A5, T12, T8, T9, T3)

Proof. By a 'state of consciousness' is understood, in the first place, at least something directly known in experience as *one* state. In accordance with A5, we can each know that such a state exists at any present moment of our experience. Any such state is, then, one existence, and hence by T12 is one term.

The admission that a certain state is a state of consciousness implies the recognition in it of something of which there is consciousness (the 'object') and of that which is conscious of it (the 'subject'). Although subject and object are distinct, they are contents of the state, and by T3 Cor. 1 are related to it, and hence by T9 they are neither separable from the state nor from one another. To admit that a certain state of consciousness is a state of a certain person is to admit that the subject of the state is that person. Thus to say that I am in a certain state is to say that I am the subject of the state.

It belongs to the meaning of 'I' that if it has reference at all, it at least refers to the subject of a *present* state of consciousness. If I have had any past states, they are admittedly mine only in so far as the subjects of these past states are all the 'same' as the subject (myself) of my present state. This implies at least continuity, *i.e.* relationship, between these states and my present state. It follows by T9 that my states of consciousness are all identical. (This is why the sense of 'I' runs through them all. There is one being which all these states are.)

But the usual step of analogy leads me to believe that there are also states of consciousness other than mine (and along with them, conscious beings other than myself). Now I would accord the description 'state of consciousness' to any one of these, solely in so far as I believe that it resembles my states of consciousness in possessing the same nature as these, *viz. consciousness*. If this signifies a real content which they possess in common, then by T8 these other states are all identical with my states. If it does not, then the resemblance between these states and mine is possible only through particular relations of resemblance. In that case it follows by T9 that these other states are all identical with mine. Thus my belief in the existence of states resembling my states of consciousness in being conscious (presupposed by my belief in the existence of other minds) implies commitment to the identity of these other states with mine. Correspondingly, if there *are* other minds, my belief in them is true, and all other states of consciousness *are* identical with mine.

It now follows that, whether there are or are not other minds, all states of consciousness (such as there are) are identical with one another. That is, all these states are one and the same being, and it is to this being that the name 'consciousness' properly applies. Since this being is identical with each state, and since I know, from my identity with each of my own states in turn, that they are alive, this being must be alive; and like each state it must be one existing term.

Comments

This theorem can be viewed, in the first place, as an unqualified rejection of the treatment of consciousness as a merely abstract feature of states of consciousness. In general, T8 and T9 show that universals cannot be abstract but must be concrete. This is not to say that a concrete universal must in practice be supposed to underlie any and every class of entities we like to dream up. In one of Plato's dialogues, *Parmenides*,[1] Socrates was asked whether mud and hair were to be regarded as forms (*i.e.* universals). What we have to remember, in any such case, is that *two* conditions are needed to ensure the significant existence of a universal for a given class. The first condition is that the members of the class should indeed have something in common. Through T9, this condition is at once satisfied for all ordinary classes. Moreover it is satisfied concretely, because it is ensured that what is in common is identical with each concrete instance, and so automatically possesses all their concrete properties. Like other ordinary classes, mud and hair would satisfy this condition. The second condition is that what is in common to the members of the class should be limited to just this class. This condition is seldom or never satisfied for any ordinary class, because, as Wittgenstein has argued,[2] it is virtually impossible to rule out borderline cases. In confirmation of this, the completed System implies the impossibility of any absolute limitation (T19). There may be one stable, self-identical being underlying experience, but it appears that no differences in experience are stable. They change, dissolve, and arise again in another form with another significance.

It will be proved later that consciousness exists necessarily and without limitation. In this case, therefore, no difficulty arises about limitation and borderline cases. Consequently T13 can be regarded not only as proving that consciousness is a concrete universal, but as the beginning of a proof that consciousness is the one stable, infinite being underlying experi-

[1] Plato, *Parmenides and Other Dialogues*, London 1961, p. 5.
[2] L. Wittgenstein, *Philosophical Investigations*, Oxford 1963, §§ 68, 69.

ence. Part II of the System in effect incorporates a proof of the existence of God, and T13 is the beginning of this proof.

12. *The Identity of Every Existence with Consciousness.* T14, T15

T14. *Every term must coexist with consciousness, and be identical with it throughout their existence.* (T13, T12, T3, A3, T2, T11)

Proof. Suppose that a certain term X is unrelated to consciousness at all times of their existence.

This supposition we shall call 'S', and consciousness we shall call 'C'. We aim at deducing from S the conclusion that X is related to C.

S is a thought occurring in my present state of consciousness. Now just as a state of consciousness is something directly known in experience as one state (see proof of T13), so a thought contained in such a state is something directly known in experience as one act. It is thus one existence, and by T12 one term. S, then, is a term.

As in T13, my present state of consciousness is related to C, and S (by T3 Cor. 1) is related to my present state, and hence (by A3) through my present state to C. (In fact it is clear that S is constituted by C, and that the relation between S and C is an essential basis of the present proof.)

The next step is to see whether X and S are related. S is about the two terms X and C, and this pair we shall write '(X, C)'.

From S it follows that S applies truly to its subject-matter, *viz.* to (X, C). But from S it also follows that X and C are unrelated. Hence by T2 transposed, X and C cannot belong to one system, nor (by D1 and D2) be one term. That is, no unity of X and C is possible. Therefore S, in applying truly to (X, C), cannot apply to (X, C) as a unit, and so can only apply (truly) to them by applying (truly) directly to X, and directly to C. In other words, since the condition of the truth of S is not possible as a *relation* between X and C, it is possible only as a *quality* or *state* of X, and, separately, a quality or state of C. (For example, we should say that X is unthinkable, rather than that X is unrelated to C.)

The direct, true application of S to X means this: that

whatever content K in S is claimed by S to hold for X, must in fact hold for X. Thus X has this content K in common with S. Hence by T3 Cor. 2, X is related to S.

We now have the two results, *viz*. X is related to S, and S is related to C. This implies by A3 that X is related to C now, *viz*. at the time of my making the supposition, since the supposition is the middle term. This contradicts the unrelatedness (at all times) which S asserts to hold between this term X and C. Thus S is self-contradictory and false.

What this proves is that there is at least some time at which *this particular term X* is related to C. But since S has been needed as a middle term between X and C, the result would not have been proved for an X for which a supposition S had not been framed. But having proved the result (that X is related to C) for this particular term X, it follows that X *can* be related to C. Moreover, this holds for *any* X, since we *can* frame a supposition S corresponding to *any* given X. It follows by T11 that X, whatever X may be, must coexist with consciousness, and be identical with it throughout their existence.

Cor. 1. Any two terms must coexist, and be related and identical throughout their existence.

Cor. 2. Any difference between terms must always be difference-in-identity.

Comments

1. In this proof it is tempting to pay primary attention to the second, more formal part, in which X is proved related to S. Having proved this, we could then add that, in a *similar way*, C could be proved related to S. In fact any term Y which we might put in place of C in S would then be proved related to S; and any two terms X and Y would be proved related (through S). The relation between X and C would then appear merely as a special case.

But all this overlooks the fact that S must be *one* term for the proof to hold. When we look into this we find that the relation of S to C is central to the whole proof, as indicated in the first part of the proof. For it is just this relation of S to consciousness which ensures that S *is* one term.

2. The provisional aim in T14 is to deduce from S the conclusion that X is related to C. When this result is reached it

is tempting to use the weak form of T11. This of course will not do, and the details of the proof at this point show just why it will not do. We actually frame an S for one (or a few) X's. We *can* frame an S for *any* X. It is just because we *can* do that there *is* an underlying relation between consciousness (C) and any X (as T11 in the strong form indicates). For X to be unthinkable (though no supposition to that effect be made) means that a certain negative category of consciousness is already applicable to X, and hence that X is thinkable and related to consciousness. This is the philosophical principle behind T14.

3. The special application of T11 to the terms X and C in T14 should indicate why the corollary of T11 is important historically. A favourite stand-by of realists and materialists is the assumption that even if a term (X) could be, and perhaps is at a certain time, related to consciousness (C), it is nevertheless possible for such a term to exist quite independently of consciousness, and to continue to exist even when consciousness no longer exists. It is just this kind of assumption that is defeated by T11 Cor.

4. In T13 and T14, some difficulty arises about applying the theory of relations, and especially T9, to particular relations in experience. For, in order to justify application, we must first ascertain that the particular relation in question is indeed a relation according to the meaning of the word 'relation' as used in the System.

Two courses are open. The first is to seek formal proof of relationship, as in T3. The trouble here is that T9 Cor. (that all continuity is identity) suggests that it is in the end not possible to understand relation clearly except in terms of identity. The success of formal proof would therefore seem to depend upon the discovery of something common to the terms. And then T8 rather than T9 becomes important, and the strength of T9 is largely lost.

A second course is open because what is normally accepted as a relation is so accepted because a real unity is believed to underlie it, and because it is normally beyond dispute that some form of unity is present. Using T9 Cor. again, we can argue that since unity is agreed to be present, continuity and identity must also be agreed to be present.

In fact the normal attitude of critics of idealism is to deny the identity of a perceived object with consciousness, while *maintaining* their relationship. For example G. E. Moore, in his essay 'The Refutation of Idealism', argued that the object of consciousness is external to consciousness, while fully accepting the existence of a relation of knowing between consciousness and its object.[1] So even if externality implied nothing more than discrepancy, the situation as envisaged by Moore is entirely destroyed by the Identity Theorem (T9). In view of this it is in practice artificial and redundant to seek formal proof of relationship. The disagreement does not lie in the premiss claiming relationship.

5. In proving the coexistence of consciousness with every term, we have not quite proved what I call the 'semi-eternal' existence of consciousness. To do this we have to prove the coexistence of consciousness not only with every term but with every existence. This further step is taken by the following theorem, T15, with which we therefore conclude the chapter.

T15. *Whatever exists must always be one term, and must always be consciousness.* (T2, T14, D1)
Proof. An existing thing or set containing any gap of unrelatedness would be at least two unrelated terms (T2 transposed). This is impossible by T14 Cor. 1. Hence any such existing thing or set is one term (D1), and hence coexists with consciousness, and is identical with it throughout their existence (T14).
Cor. So long as anything exists, consciousness exists.

13. *The Necessary Existence of Consciousness.* T16, T17

T16. *Something must always exist.*
Proof. Suppose that (at a certain time) there is not anything in existence.
To make a supposition is not to conceive that *someone imagines* the stated condition to hold, it is to conceive the stated condition as actually holding (in order to explore what follows from its holding). In the above supposition, what is conceived as actually holding, *i.e.* as being the case, is that (at a certain time)

[1] G. E. Moore, *Philosophical Studies*, London 1922, pp. 24-7.

there is not anything in existence. It is conceived as a real state of affairs which, for example, would exclude the existence of any stars, planets, or human beings. But a real state of affairs is something existing. Thus if indeed it were the case that not anything existed, this condition would be something existing, a counter-example of itself. The supposition is therefore self-contradictory, and something must always exist.

Comments

Although the principle upon which T16 depends is logically self-evident, it is important to isolate it. Any proposition can be asserted. To assert it is to claim its truth, *i.e.* that the things or entities singled out by the proposition are as the proposition states them to be. This is an affirmative claim. To negate anything is by implication to affirm that negation. I call this the principle of the 'affirmativeness' of negation, in brief the 'AN' principle.

Because any negation is also an affirmation it at once becomes conceivable that what is negated may include, or even coincide with, what is affirmed. In either case a contradiction results, and we have what is known as a 'reflexive paradox'. The paradoxical proposition is implicitly or explicitly about the positive conditions demanded for its truth; and because it is negative, it denies the existence of its own conditions of truth, producing the contradiction. In a universal negation of existence, such as the supposition in T16, the proposition cannot avoid implicitly denying the existence of its own conditions of truth.

Because the supposition in T16 involves a reflexive paradox, a critic might well argue that the supposition should be handled according to the standard method of avoiding reflexive paradoxes, *viz.* by applying rules which limit the scope of a proposition to subject-matter outside its conditions of truth. The effect would be to rule out the supposition in T16 as meaningless. We would then be denied the logical right to make such a supposition.

If the supposition were meaningless, it would certainly not express anything true, since a true proposition is at least meaningful. Accordingly there could not be any fact making the supposition true, *i.e.* there could not be any fact making it true that there is not anything in existence. And this leaves, as the only possible alternative, that there must always be something in existence, which is exactly what T16 claims. So if the proof of T16 is criticised in this manner, the criticism itself constitutes an alternative proof of T16. The theorem itself stands, whether or not the criticism of its proof is valid.

As pointed out in ch. 8, difference-in-identity is unavoidable, because the ordinary categories of separation lead to contradiction. The standard treatment of reflexive paradoxes preserves these faulty categories, by imposing separations of type or of language-levels. As a consequence, such a method of solution is always threatened by the possibility of new outbreaks of contradiction. A final solution is therefore possible only if separation (as a category of thought) is first replaced by difference-in-identity. Now difference-in-identity and reflexiveness are forms of the same principle. So a solution of the reflexive paradoxes should be sought not by eliminating the associated reflexive structures, but by eliminating mistaken applications of negation. (See the discussions of suppression in ch. 8 and in ch. 14.)

T17. *Consciousness must always exist.* (T16, T15)
   Proof. By T16 something must always exist. But by T15 this something, whatever it is at any time, must be consciousness. It follows that consciousness must always exist.

Comments
   Let us not minimise the claim of T17. It claims the unconditionally necessary existence of consciousness. How is this possible, in view of the fact that consciousness is first introduced (in A5) as if existing only contingently? The answer to this is that we do not know at the start that the existence of consciousness *is* strictly contingent, we know only that its existence is given in experience. The fact of its being given in experience simply fails to determine whether its existence is contingent or necessary. To infer the contingency of a proposition from the fact that we know it (now) only from experience, is to infer the absence of its necessity from the absence of our (present) knowledge that it is necessary. Yet many philosophers regularly make such an inference.

We know that X exists necessarily by knowing that its non-existence is impossible, and we know the non-existence of X to be impossible by proving the non-existence of X to be self-contradictory. In effect, this is what we have done in T17. If there had been any time at which consciousness had not existed, then by T15 Cor. transposed nothing would have existed at that time, which is proved self-contradictory in T16.

14. Matter and the Infinity of Consciousness. T18, T19

T18. *No non-conscious thing can exist.* (T15)

Proof. If a thing were non-conscious in any respect, it would be discrepant from consciousness, and hence non-identical with it. This is impossible by T15.

Comments

In T18 and T19 we finally reach an account of the relation (or non-relation) between consciousness and matter, and in consequence a resolution of the issue between idealism and materialism. With respect to this issue, the importance of T18 is that it eliminates matter, and the importance of T19 is that it states the positive consequence for consciousness of the elimination of matter. The comments on T18 and T19 therefore explore respectively the negative and positive sides of one and the same situation.

By T9 transposed, a thing non-conscious in any respect would not only be discrepant from consciousness, but simply different from it and unrelated to it. It would be non-conscious through and through, and in its very nature. There could be no compromise, such as that it could have qualities perceivable by a consciousness. We recall the case of the two unrelated terms in the proof of T2. Not only would a non-conscious thing (or anything related to it) be unrelated to consciousness itself, it would be unrelated to anything related to consciousness, such as states and acts of consciousness, objects of consciousness, and conscious beings. Whether a thing is non-conscious in its nature, or merely in some superficial respect, the result is the same: it is not in the same universe as consciousness.

Traditionally the word used for something non-conscious in its nature has been 'matter'. This meaning of 'matter' is implicit in the use of the words 'materialism' and 'idealism'. It is the reason why the two views denoted by these words are opposed and incompatible. While keeping in principle to this negative sense of 'matter', I shall admit a weaker and correspondingly broader meaning of the word, *viz.* anything in *any* respect non-conscious. But even with this weaker meaning, T9 proves that any material thing is totally unrelated to consciousness; and T18 (through T15) then proves the non-existence of anything material.

Once the total unrelatedness of matter to consciousness has been recognised, philosophers have often gone on to suspect the non-existence of matter, on the grounds that it is idle to believe in the existence of something which, in the nature of the case, can in no way be known or otherwise related to us.

Belief in the existence of matter is normally defended on the apparently innocent basis that something beyond consciousness is needed to explain the involuntariness of our perceptions. But if the expression 'beyond consciousness' is taken seriously, the unrelatedness of matter to consciousness follows (by T9), and matter becomes totally unable to explain *any* feature of our perceptions. Not only is the reason for believing in the existence of matter destroyed, but in view of T18 the existence of matter becomes impossible.

The only escape is to modify the concept of matter in such a way that it does not negate consciousness. Above, I have accepted the traditional meaning of 'matter' at least in so far as it involves some negation of consciousness. For matter in the modified sense (not involving any negation of consciousness) a different word or expression will therefore be needed. I shall use one or other of the expressions 'perceptible things' or 'physical things', according to which is the more relevant.

Confusion between perceptible things and material things has led to an absurd perpetuation of the philosophical disaster of dualism. The climax of this disaster has been a succession of attempts to solve the mind-body problem, without first coping with the logical consequences of assuming the body to be material.

Unfortunately we commonly assume that physical bodies are material without formulating the assumption, and in the belief that we have in fact not made it. We effectively assume materialism whenever we assume different things to be discrepant and hence non-identical; and this we are continually doing, for it belongs to our standard way of conceiving difference. It is taken for granted most of all in our thinking about physical things, but also in most thinking about consciousness. The reason why idealism comes to be discredited is not that it is illogical in itself, but that our way of thinking about the issue between idealism and materialism is itself materialistic.

Granted the reasonableness of belief in the existence of physical things, they cannot be material, and must therefore be forms of consciousness. If we describe them as 'external', we must not allow this word to imply simple difference or discrepancy from any form of consciousness (such as ours). Physical things are not *factually* external to us. But there is a modified sense in which they may be said to be external, *viz.* in the sense of externalisation (for us) due to the operation of our categories of thought. The reason why our categories externalise physical things for us is that the *concept of matter* has a central place among our categories.

The concept of matter operates in accordance with the definition which I have given for 'matter', *viz.* in a way which is at least partially exclusive of consciousness. I do not mean by this that any ideal exclusion of consciousness from the objects of the category is achieved. This occurs only with mathematical objects, and this is why we feel that the objects of pure mathematics are mental and not real. In so far as the objects of the category are recognised as still perceptible or as causally underlying perception, the operation of negating is only to *suppress* consciousness from the objects (for us). This makes these objects *appear* as external to us, and at the same time as basically devoid of consciousness, *i.e.* as material.

T19. *Consciousness is infinite.* (T18)

Proof. The meaning of 'infinite' operative in the theorem is as follows: something is infinite if and only if it is not absolutely limited, *i.e.* not limited by anything not itself.

By T18, nothing can exist which is not consciousness in some

form. It follows that consciousness cannot be limited by anything not itself, since there *is* nothing not itself so to limit it.
That is, consciousness is infinite.

Cor. Consciousness can be limited only by itself.

Comments

We begin with the notion of self-limitation introduced by the
corollary, and move on to a positive notion of infinity.

It has already been explained that we use the word 'matter'
for anything in any way not conscious. It is only matter,
therefore, that could constitute an absolute limit to consciousness. We could therefore view T19 as a simple consequence of
the non-existence of matter.

Since matter itself does not exist, the limitations from which
we suffer are not to be ascribed to matter. We can ascribe them
only to the *concept* of matter (as expressed in the definition),
i.e. to the form of consciousness through which belief in the
existence of matter is possible and can become effective.
Limitations accordingly become effective through consciousness
itself, *i.e.* they are ultimately self-limitations, in accordance with
the corollary of T19.

Given that limitation is a relation (between the limiting
agent and the subject of limitation), there is a short way to the
conception of self-limitation through T9. For the relation
between limiting agent and subject of limitation implies their
identity, *i.e.* what limits the subject is the subject itself.

This simple reduction of all limitation to self-limitation is
implausible in practice, because many of our worst limitations
stem from limitation in space and time, where the so-called
'agent of limitation' appears to be sheer emptiness or nothingness. *Is* limitation in these cases a relation between what is
limited and an agent of limitation? The natural account of the
limitation of a thing in space is not that the surrounding
emptiness blocks the thing's further extension, but that the
thing by its own nature fails to extend further.

The difficulty with this is that in denying that the surrounding space is anything positive which can serve as a limiting
agent, we automatically give up the premiss that the surrounding space *is* what limits the thing. What does limit it, then?
Since the limitation is not from without, it must be from within,

by the thing's own nature. This already looks very much like self-limitation; and even if a way is found to avoid this, it at least admits that limitation is a relation between what is limited and something real which limits it.

But is it in fact true that space and time are pure negations? If they were, they would present no obstacle at all to movement. Again, if they were pure negations, *i.e.* absolute nothingness, they could not be distinguished into parts which could be measured and compared in size. In space and time we have concrete illustrations of the truth of T16, *viz.* that absolute nothingness is an impossibility. Space and time, along with their physical contents, must be real, and since they are real they must, by T15, be forms of consciousness. We are profoundly deceived about this, because of the way in which the concept of matter operates. Not only does it externalise and materialise physical things, it does just the same with space and time. The result is not only the illusion of physical things as material, but also the illusion of space and time as real states of emptiness existing independently of any consciousness, in which physical things exist and move. This is the space and time which Kant reduced to contradiction in his First Antinomy.[1]

Materialistic thought thus generates deeper and deeper illusions for itself; and the objects of these illusions, *viz.* matter, are non-entities. But corresponding to the non-existent material structures purporting to be beyond consciousness, there are the real structures, within consciousness, of the illusions themselves. These structures are the work of the *concept* of matter, the reality in us underlying the fictitious *matter*. Physical things could be described as the reality *different from* us, underlying the fictitious *matter*. The function of perception should be to reveal the identity in this difference between physical things and ourselves. But the concept of matter thwarts this function by suppressing the identity.

In perception as elsewhere, consciousness is related to its object. Therefore (by T9) consciousness is identical with its object, even though our concept of matter suppresses the revelation of the identity to us in perception. Consequently all consciousness of objects is potentially consciousness of itself, *i.e.*

[1] I. Kant, *Critique of Pure Reason*, tr. N. Kemp Smith, London 1964, pp. 396-8.

self-consciousness. To be self-conscious is not to be favoured by a special form of consciousness over and above consciousness of ordinary objects; one is already (potentially at least) self-conscious *in* being conscious of ordinary objects. This sort of self-consciousness I call 'self-consciousness in objects', or 'objective self-consciousness'. Such a consciousness extends beyond the limits imposed by conceiving objects as material, into the heart of the object itself. For this reason objective self-consciousness is a form of infinity which is positive, and not defined merely in terms of removal of limitation. And this positive infinite can become an integral part of our experience, once we free our categories of the concept of matter.